Jon Scieszka's Trucktown
on Reading abcs

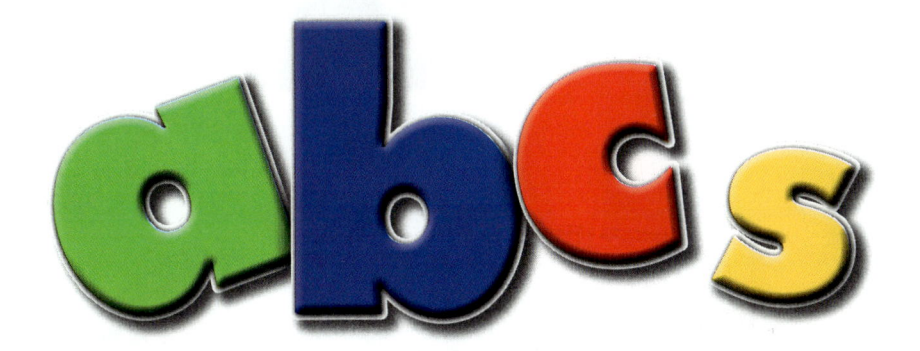

CHARACTERS AND ENVIRONMENTS DEVELOPED BY THE

dESiGN garage

David Shannon   **Loren Long**   **David Gordon**

ILLUSTRATION CREW:
Executive Producer: Keytoon, Inc. in association with Animagic S.L.
Creative supervisor: Sergio Pablos
Drawings by: Juan Pablo Navas
Color by: Isabel Nadal

PEARSON

Glenview, Illinois • Boston, Massachusetts • Chandler, Arizona • Upper Saddle River, New Jersey

Copyright © by Pearson Education, Inc., or its affiliates. All rights reserved. Printed in Mexico. This publication is protected by copyright, and permission should be obtained from the publisher prior to any prohibited reproduction, storage in a retrieval system, or transmission in any form or by any means, electronic, mechanical, photocopying, recording, or likewise. For information regarding permissions, write to Pearson Curriculum Rights & Permissions, One Lake Street, Upper Saddle River, New Jersey 07458.

Pearson® is a trademark, in the U.S. and/or in other countries, of Pearson plc or its affiliates.

Scott Foresman® is a trademark, in the U.S and/or in other countries, of Pearson Education, Inc., or its affiliates.

TRUCKTOWN and JON SCIESZKA'S TRUCKTOWN and design are trademarks of JRS Worldwide, LLC

ISBN 13: 978-0-328-42061-2
ISBN 10: 0-328-42061-1

16 17

Gabriella

Dan

Rita

Max

Pat and Lucy

Melvin

Pete

Big Rig

Kat

Jack

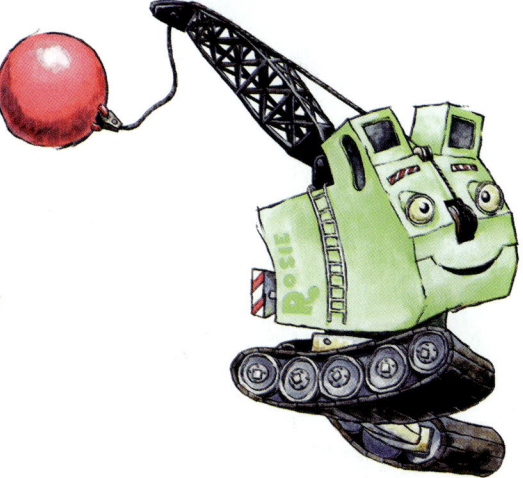

Rosie

Izzy

Ted

Aa
Action

Bb
Big Rig

Cc
Cabs

Dd

Dan

Ee
Explore

Ff
Fun

Gg
Gabriella

Hh
Highway

Ii
Izzy

Jj
Jack

Kk
Kat

Ll

Lucy

Mm

Max and Melvin

Nn
Noisy

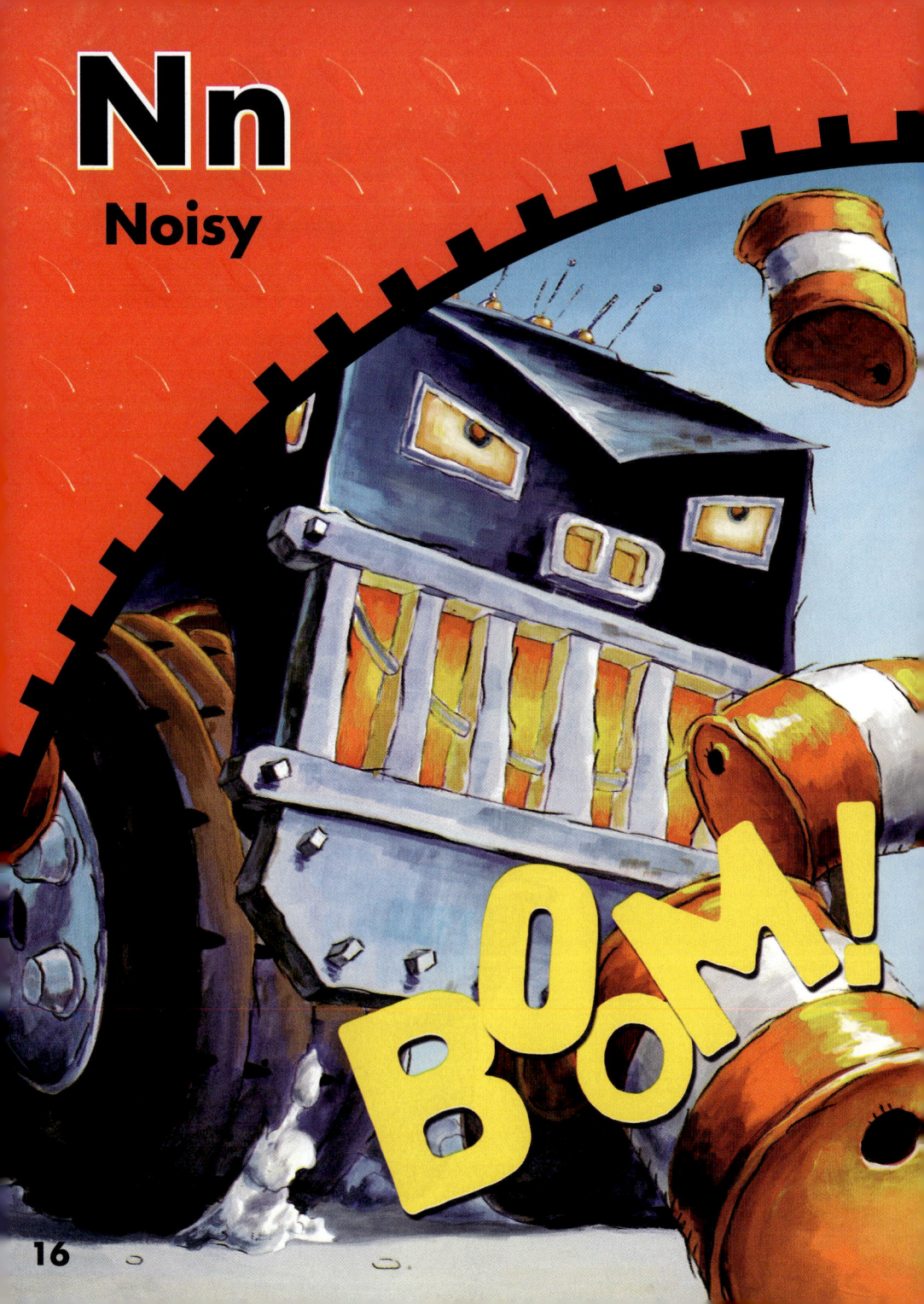

16

Oo
On

Pp
Pete and Pat

Qq
Quick

Rr
Rosie and Rita

Ss
Signs

Tt

Ted

Uu
Under

Vv
Vroom

22

Ww
Work

Xx
Exit

Yy
Yard

Zz
Zig and Zag